MASS
JOURNAL

DynamicCatholic.com
Be Bold. Be Catholic.®

MASS JOURNAL

Printed in the United States of America.[1]

ISBN (Hard Cover): 978-0-9841318-4-6

For more information on this title and other books and CDs
available through the Dynamic Catholic Book Program,
please visit: www.DynamicCatholic.com

The Dynamic Catholic Institute
5081 Olympic Blvd • Erlanger, Kentucky 41018
Phone: 1–859–980–7900
Email: info@DynamicCatholic.com

Introduction

The Origin of the Idea

Many years ago, I was speaking to a group of young people and I encouraged them to get a small journal, take it to Mass with them, and ask God to show them one way they could become a-better-version-of-themselves in the coming week. A couple of weeks later, I received a journal in the mail from one of the students who had heard me share the idea . . . and I started to use it. That small journal changed my whole experience of the Mass.

Each Sunday, when I walk into Mass I pray, *God, Show me one way in this Mass I can become the-best-version-of-myself this week!* God never fails to respond to this prayer. So, each week I write down the one way I sense God is challenging me to grow, change, and become all he created me to be.

Today, I can look back at several Mass Journals. If you name a month and a year, I can tell you what I was struggling with in my life at that time by picking up the Mass Journal for that year. I can also tell you how God brought me through that period in my life. This knowledge of where we have come from, this spiritual continuity, is very powerful. It gives us hope in times of discouragement, and joy in times of sorrow.

This Mass Journal has also become a very powerful aid in my daily prayer. Often I take it to daily prayer and reflect on several of the short entries, one at a time, slowly and thoughtfully. They become a starting point for my conversation with God in prayer.

Our Lives Change When Our Habits Change

A Mass Journal is a life-changing habit for an individual, a marriage, a family, a parish, and the whole Church.

As an individual, take it to Mass, write down the one thing you sense God is saying to you that week, and date your entry. Then use your Mass Journal in daily prayer and allow it to stimulate your conversation with God.

In your marriage, take a few minutes on Sunday night to discuss what you each heard God saying to you and what you are working on during the coming week. Then pray for each other, keeping these intentions specifically in mind.

In your family, on the way home from church, ask your children, "What did God say to you at church today?" Make it a habit—simply by asking the question you are teaching them to listen to the voice of God in their lives.

To test the idea I asked a friend who is a Catholic school teacher to ask her second-grade students, first thing each Monday morning, what God said to them at church on Sunday. She said she couldn't do that, explaining that most of the children don't go to church on Sunday. I encouraged her not to worry about that and to ask the question anyway. Three months later, at the parent-teacher conferences, eight parents talked about how they had stopped going to Mass some time ago, but this year their children had started asking them to take them to church. They wanted to hear what God was going to say to them, they told their parents.

In your parish, get everyone a Mass Journal. Perhaps after the homily, your priest could encourage everyone to take a quiet moment and write down the one thing God said to them in the Mass so far. We could then spend the rest of the Mass praying about how you can begin to live that one thing in the coming week.

Listening to the Voice of God

It seems to me that our lives change for the better only when we listen to the voice of God and respond to what we hear with courage and generosity.

Imagine every person in your parish coming to church on Sunday with a Mass Journal, listening to the voice of God in their lives, looking for the one way they could become the-best-version-of-themselves in the coming week.

Imagine the conversations you would have with your children, your spouse, your friends, and your pastor about the one thing you are each working on. Imagine the energy. Imagine the renewal. Imagine the possibilities.

Now take it a step further: Imagine every Catholic in America coming to church on Sunday with a Mass Journal, actively seeking the one way they could become a-better-version-of-themselves this week.

We do have problems as a Church—we are hypnotized by complexity—but I believe that one simple habit like this can turn the tide for the Catholic Church in America. Get people listening to the voice of God in their lives and something incredible will happen.

Many will say that this idea is too simple. Others will say we need to focus on catechesis and the sacraments. These are important, but until people are listening to the voice of God in their lives they are simply incapable of absorbing the Scriptures, the Sunday homily, CCD class, adult education courses, great Catholic books, and the phenomenal beauty of the sacraments.

But once people are listening to the voice of God in their lives, they become sponges for everything else the Church has to offer. Teaching people to listen to the voice of God in their lives is a game changer for the Church. The Mass Journal is a simple and practical tool to teach Catholics how to listen to the voice of God and become continuous learners in their spiritual lives.

Could one simple habit transform the Catholic Church in the United States? Could it also transform your life, marriage, parish, career, spiritual life, school, business, and your appreciation of Catholicism?

Yes. As disarmingly simple as it may seem, you could be holding the key to transforming the Catholic Church in America. I wonder if we are humble enough as a Church to embrace such a simple strategy as a way forward?

When seventy percent of American Catholics don't come to church on Sunday, isn't it time someone did something? We think it is, and we hope you will join us in our efforts.

I invite you to take this small journal to Mass with you each Sunday. On your way to church join me in this simple prayer, *God, Show me one way in this Mass I can become a better-version-of-myself this week!* Avoid the temptation to write copious notes. Just write down that one way you sense God is calling you to grow, and date your entry.

After a year, you will be able to flick through the pages of this journal and see how you have grown. Ten years from now, you will have ten of these small journals and together they will tell the story of your spiritual journey throughout those years.

There is genius in Catholicism. Let's rediscover it together.

Matthew Kelly

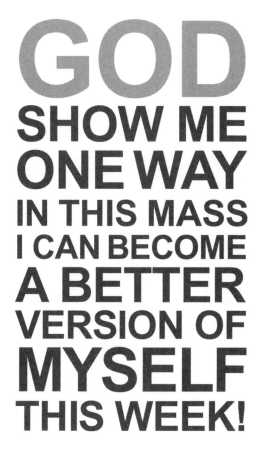

1 There are 1.2 billion Catholics in the world. There are sixty-seven million Catholics in America—that's at least fifteen million more people than it takes to elect an American president. And every single day the Catholic Church feeds, houses, and clothes more people, takes care of more sick people, visits more prisoners, and educates more people than any other institution on the face of the earth could ever hope to.

2 There is genius in Catholicism, if we will just take the time and make the effort to humbly explore it. If you and I are not part of the solution, we are part of the problem. If sixty-seven million Catholics in the United States stepped it up a notch, something incredible would happen. So let's decide, here and now, today, to begin to explore the genius of our faith, to be part of the solution, and to step it up a notch.

Rediscover Catholicism

3 Two thousand years ago, a small group of people captured the attention and intrigued the imagination of the entire Western world. At first, these people were thought to be of no consequence, the followers of a man most considered to be nothing more than an itinerant preacher. But when this man was put to death, a dozen of his followers rose up and began telling people about his life and teachings. They began telling the story of Jesus Christ. They were not the educated elite of their time, they had no political or social status, they were not wealthy, and they had no worldly authority, yet from the very beginning people were joining this quiet revolutionary group one hundred at a time. This small group of people were the first Christians. They were the original followers of Jesus of Nazareth and the first members of what we know today as the Catholic Church.

4 The story of Jesus Christ is the most powerful in history and has directly or indirectly influenced every noble aspect of modern civilization. But amid the hustle and bustle of our daily lives, it is easy to become distracted and distance ourselves from this story. From time to time, someone comes along who reminds us of the spellbinding power the Gospel has when it is actually lived.

5 The first Christians were not perfect; nor were the saints. They lived in communities that were torn by strife in ways remarkably similar to what we are experiencing today, and they struggled with the brokenness of their own humanity in the same way you and I do. But they were dedicated to the basics. The first Christians intrigued the people of their time. So did the saints, and so do ordinary people who embrace the Christian life today. In the great majority of cases they don't do anything spectacular. For the most part they commit themselves to doing simple things spectacularly well and with great love, and that intrigues people. We need to intrigue the people of our time in the same ways. Whom does your life intrigue? Not with spectacular accomplishments, but simply by the way you live, love, and work.

6 God always wants our future to be bigger than our past. Not equal to our past, but bigger, better, brighter, and more significant. God wants your future and my future, and the future of the Church, to be bigger than the past. It is this bigger future that we need to envision. One of the most incredible abilities God has given the human person is the ability to dream. We are able to look into the future and imagine something better than today, and then return to the present and work to make that richly imagined future a reality. Who is doing this for the Church? For many years I have been reflecting on a single verse from Proverbs. It never ceases to ignite my passion for the Church. "Where there is no vision, the people will perish." (Proverbs 28:19) I have found this to be true in every area of life. In a country where there is no vision, the people will perish. In a marriage where there is no vision, people will perish. In a business, a school, or a family where there is no vision, the people will perish.

7 Now is a time when we all need to rediscover Catholicism. I try to rediscover it every day, and when I seek in earnest to do so I am never disappointed. When I am able to set my ego and personal agenda aside, more often than not I am left in awe. Catholicism is old. But let me ask you a question. If you had an ancient treasure map, would you throw it away just because it was old? No. The age of the map doesn't matter. What matters is whether or not it leads to treasure. Catholicism is a treasure map: It may be old, but it still leads to treasure. Let's rediscover it together, and help others to do the same.

8 The human heart is on a quest for happiness. Every person yearns for happiness like the desert yearns for rain. You have a desire for happiness; I have a desire for happiness. This desire is universal, common to every member of the human family. We simply desire to be happy, and we act from this desire. We often do things that we think will make us happy, only to discover that they end up making us miserable. This is often because we confuse pleasure with happiness. And sometimes long-term misery comes disguised as short-term pleasure.

9 I believe God wants us to be happy. I believe God gave us this yearning for happiness that constantly preoccupies our hearts. It seems he has placed this yearning within each human heart as a spiritual navigational instrument designed to lead us to our destiny. God himself is the author of our desire for happiness. The philosophy of Christ is the ultimate philosophy of human happiness. It isn't just a way of life; it is *the* way of life. At the same time, the philosophy of Christ is one of self-donation. This is the great paradox of God's teaching. In our misguided adventures, we may catch glimpses of happiness as we live outside of the philosophy of Christ. You may even taste happiness for a moment living a life contrary to the philosophy of Christ, but these are stolen moments. They may seem real, but they are just shadows of something infinitely greater.

10 Before Christmas last year, I saw a Jewish scholar interviewed on television. The topic of discussion was the influence Jesus has exerted on human history. In summary, the scholar concluded, "The impact this man has had on human history is undeniable. Because of this man we call Jesus, the world will never again be the same. Because of Jesus, men and women will never think the same. Regardless of whether or not we believe he was the Son of God, because of this man who walked the earth two thousand years ago, men and women will never live the same, will never be the same."

11 The life of Jesus Christ is indelibly engraved upon history; neither the erosion of time nor the devastating and compounding effects of evil have been able to erase his influence. Some people thought he was crazy; others considered him a misfit, a troublemaker, a rebel. He was condemned as a criminal, yet his life and teachings reverberate throughout history. He saw things differently, and he had no respect for the status quo. You can praise him, disagree with him, quote him, disbelieve him, glorify him, or vilify him. About the only thing you cannot do is ignore him, and that is a lesson that every age learns in its own way. You can't ignore Jesus, because he changed things. He is the single greatest agent of change in human history. He made the lame walk, taught the simple, set captives free, gave sight to the blind, fed the hungry, healed the sick, comforted the afflicted, afflicted the comfortable, and in all of these, captured the imagination of every generation.

_____

_____

_____

_____

_____

_____

_____

_____

_____

_____

_____

_____

12 The *Catechism of the Catholic Church* wastes no time in addressing this truth. The opening point of Chapter One, Section One, reads, "The desire for God is written in the human heart, because man is created by God and for God; and God never ceases to draw man to himself. Only in God will man find the truth and happiness he never stops yearning for."

_____

_____

_____

_____

_____

_____

_____

_____

_____

_____

_____

_____

13 God created us with legitimate needs. We all have legitimate physical, emotional, intellectual, and spiritual needs. The most basic understanding of these legitimate needs comes from considering our relationship to food, water, and oxygen. To eat and drink are legitimate needs. If you don't eat and drink, you will die. If you don't breathe, you will die even faster. God gave us these needs for a reason. When we hear them calling to us, we hear the voice of God.

14 It is through prayer, reflection, the Scriptures, the grace of the sacraments, the wisdom of the Church, and the guidance of the Holy Spirit that we discover and walk the path that God is calling us to walk. In our own way, we all seek out our individual destiny. Drawn by our yearning for happiness, we may seek to experience pleasure, possessions, and even power, but the world and all it has to offer can never content the human heart. God alone can satisfy the deepest cravings of our hearts.

15 There are certain disciplines that are associated with the lifestyle of an athlete that could also be compared with the lifestyle of a Christian. Athletes abide by certain diets and adhere to certain training regimens. They don't stay out all night partying, because they know they have to wake early the next morning for training. All these are part of an athlete's lifestyle. So it is with the life of a Christian. There are disciplines and practices that must be embraced and respected if we are to walk faithfully along the path of salvation, fulfill our destiny, become better-versions-of-ourselves each day, and enjoy the happiness God wants to fill us with. Your journey with God will require more discipline than any other quest you will pursue in this life.

16 For the first Christians, Christianity was a lifestyle. They shared a common life. Living in a community, they often worked together, prayed together, and studied the Scriptures together. Their faith was the center of their lives; it affected everything they did. They shared meals together, played together, and cared for each other in sickness. They allowed the principles of the Gospel to guide them in the activities of their daily lives. They comforted each other in their afflictions and challenged each other to live the Gospel more fully. There was unity and continuity between their professional lives and their family lives, between their social lives and their lives as members of the Church. They allowed the Holy Spirit to guide them in all they did. Then, at the pinnacle of their common life, they celebrated Eucharist together.

_____

_____

_____

_____

_____

_____

_____

_____

_____

_____

_____

_____

_____

17 Catholicism is not merely a religion, or a sect, or a set of rules. When small minds and smaller spirits try to capture the essence of Catholicism, this is often what they tend to conclude. But Catholicism is *more* than a religion. It is more than just another movement. The essence of Catholicism is not sin, punishment, duty, or obligation, and it is more than a set of lifeless rules and regulations. Catholicism is more. It is more than most people think and more than most Catholics ever experience. The essence of Catholicism is dynamic transformation. You cannot become more like Jesus Christ and at the same time stay as you are. To be Catholic means to be striving to live the Gospel, to be striving to become more like Jesus Christ. It is this dynamic approach to transformation that animates the human person—physically, emotionally, intellectually, and spiritually—and allows us to experience life "to the fullest." (John 10:10) When are you most fully alive? When you are changing and growing and exploring all you are capable of becoming.

_____

_____

_____

_____

_____

_____

_____

_____

_____

_____

_____

_____

_____

18 G. K. Chesterton wrote, "Christianity has not been tried and found wanting; it has been found difficult and not tried." This is particularly true of Catholicism. Of all the many people I know who have rejected Catholicism, or who are critical of it, I do not know a single person who has truly explored and embraced the Catholic lifestyle. If you *humbly* open your heart, mind, and soul to the genius of Catholicism, you will not find it wanting.

19 How I wish that when people discovered you or I are Catholic, they could immediately conclude that we are honest, hardworking, generous, loving, joyful, compassionate, temperate, humble, disciplined, prayerful, and generally in love with life. You wouldn't need too many people like this to develop a positive reputation for Catholicism in a local community. I pray that God raises them up. I pray that God will transform you and me into Catholics of that caliber. All it will take to radically alter the way Catholics are perceived in society today is for you and me to become . . . honest, hardworking, generous, loving, joyful, compassionate, temperate, humble, disciplined, prayerful, and generally in love with life.

_____

_____

_____

_____

_____

_____

_____

_____

_____

_____

_____

_____

20 In every age, the Church experiences problems and difficulties. Our time is no different. The solution to the problems that plague our lives and the Church is unchanging and singular. The problems are many; the solution is solitary. Personal holiness is the answer to every problem. In every situation in my life, in every problem, in every difficulty, I know that if I allow the values and principles of the Gospel to guide me, it will turn out for the best.

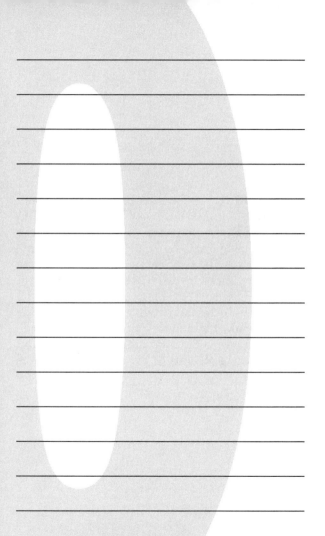

21 In every age, there are a small number of men and women who are prepared to turn their backs on popular culture and personal gain to embrace heroically the life Jesus outlines in the Gospels. These people fashion Catholicism into a lifestyle, they listen attentively to the voice of God in their lives, and they passionately pursue their personal adventure of salvation. As a result, they capture the attention and the imaginations of everyone who crosses their path.

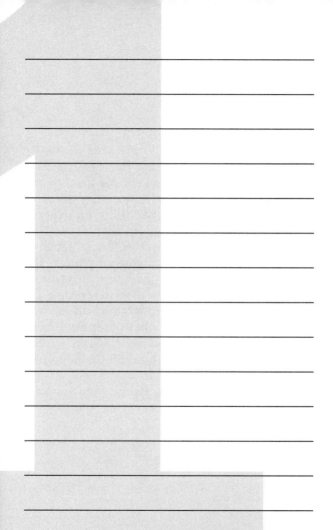

_____

_____

_____

_____

_____

_____

_____

_____

_____

_____

_____

_____

_____

22 When making a decision, the Native American people used to ask themselves how their decision today would affect their people seven generations from now. One hundred years from now, none of us will be here. Let us always remember that in the whole scheme of things, the Church is on loan to us for a very brief time. And yet in that brief time we determine the Church our children and grandchildren will inherit. In this way, God has appointed us to take care of the vineyard—the Church. This is a responsibility we should take seriously. In Matthew's Gospel (Mt. 21:33–41) we are given a vision of what happens when servants are overcome with pride and arrogance.

23 As Catholics, the one thing we do more than anything else is celebrate. Everything the Church does is centered around a celebration. We celebrate life. We celebrate the changing seasons with the richness of the Church's calendar. We celebrate excellence by honoring as saints the heroes of our faith. We celebrate birth and eternal life with baptism and burial. We celebrate truth, beauty, and goodness by seeking them out wherever they are to be found and honoring them in our everyday lives. We celebrate Christmas and Easter. We celebrate pilgrimage—our common journey and our own individual journeys. We celebrate salvation. We celebrate forgiveness with reconciliation. We celebrate total dedication to the service of God's people with Holy Orders. We celebrate education. We celebrate communion with God and community with the Mass. We celebrate unity by seeking to bridge the gap. We celebrate love with marriage. We celebrate . . .

_____

_____

_____

_____

_____

_____

_____

_____

_____

_____

_____

_____

24 I believe the best way to defend life is to celebrate life. I believe the best way to celebrate life is to live our own lives to the fullest—to embrace life with arms wide open, to lay our lives enthusiastically at the service of humanity, to love deeply the people who cross our paths, and above all, to embrace our God. Life should never be wasted—not one moment—because life is precious. You can celebrate anything you wish. You can celebrate life and faith. You can celebrate love and honesty, mercy and forgiveness, kindness and generosity. You can celebrate truth, beauty, goodness, and redemption. On the other hand, you can celebrate destruction and paganism. You can celebrate hatred and violence, selfishness and greed, contempt and disrespect. You can celebrate perversion, corruption, pride, deceit, and condemnation. But one thing is certain: We become what we celebrate. This is the one immutable truth found in the life of every person who has ever lived. We become what we celebrate. It is true not only of the life of a person but also of the life of a family. It is true of the life of a nation, and it is true of the life of the Church.

25 Several years ago, my brother Nathan was living in Japan for a year as an exchange student. During that time, I received a letter from him with a photograph he had taken of what seemed to be the courtyard of an ancient Japanese garden. In the middle of the courtyard was an almond tree in full bloom. Nathan has always been a talented photographer, but what really captured my attention was a quotation he had written on the back of the photograph. The quotation was from the writings of Greco, the famed Greek-born Spanish painter. It read: "I said to the almond tree, 'Sister, speak to me about God,' and the almond tree blossomed."

_____

_____

_____

_____

_____

_____

_____

_____

_____

_____

_____

_____

26 Only one thing is necessary for Catholicism to flourish—authentic lives. Throughout history, wherever you find men and women genuinely striving to live the Christian life, the Church has always blossomed. If we wish to speak effectively to the modern world about God, the Christian life, and Catholicism, we must be thriving, blossoming, and flourishing in that life. The best way to speak about God is to thrive in the life he calls us to live. The authentic life begins with the simple desire to be who God created us to be and cooperate with God by playing the part he has designed for us in human history. The adventure of salvation begins when we stop asking, "What's in it for me?" and turn humbly to God in our hearts and ask, *How may I serve? What work do you wish for me to do with my life? What is your will for my life?*

27 God calls each of us to live an authentic life. He has designed this life to perfectly integrate our legitimate needs, our deepest desires, and our unique talents. The more intimately and harmoniously these three are related, the more you become truly yourself.

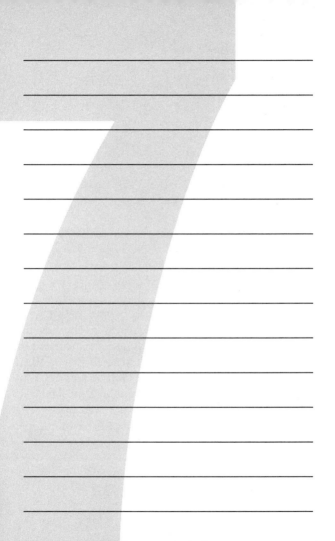

28 A man's work may be to collect the trash, but if he does it well, and hour by hour turns to God in his heart and says, *Father, I offer you this hour of work as a prayer for my neighbor Karen, who is struggling with cancer . . . or in thanksgiving for my wife and children,* then he has truly discovered and is living the words "pray constantly" (1 Thessalonians 5:17). He has transformed an hour of work into an hour of prayer. Through his work he has grown in intimacy with God and neighbor, and he has become a-better-version-of-himself. The attitude with which we approach our work is crucial. The transformation of ordinary activities into prayer is the very essence of the inner life. Every activity of our day can lead us to experience God. Learn to foster the interior life in this way and you will live a life uncommon in the midst of common circumstances.

29 We are called to live holy lives and this is something we should strive for as Christians, but let me be very clear that this holiness is not something that we can attain for ourselves. In truth, holiness is something God does in us and not something we achieve. And yet at the same time, God is the perfect gentleman: He invites us to participate in his life, but never forces himself upon us. He wants our consent, he wants to be invited into our hearts and lives, but much more than consent and invitation he desires our loving cooperation. God yearns for us to be coworkers with him in this work of holiness. It is this dynamic collaboration between God and man that brings delight to God. The North Star is the only star in the sky that never moves; it remains constant and unwavering, and therefore is a true guide. In the same way, God's call to live a holy life never changes. In a world of rapid and constant change, it is what is unchanging that allows us to make sense of change. The ideas you encounter may change, your emotions may change, but God's call to live a holy life never changes.

_____

_____

_____

_____

_____

_____

_____

_____

_____

_____

_____

_____

30 Holiness and renewal are inseparably linked. Where there is holiness the Church has always thrived. If the Church is not thriving there is one primary reason for that... and when you and I begin to take God's call to live holy lives seriously, the Church will begin to thrive in new and exciting ways. Holiness is compatible with every state in life. Married people are called to live holy lives just as much as monks and nuns. Sexual intimacy is a profound gift from God and an instrument of holiness. The riches of this world have value only inasmuch as they help us fulfill our essential purpose. If we own them, they can be powerful tools that help us live holy lives. If they own us, they will prevent us from becoming the-best-version-of-ourselves. The rich are called to live holy lives by using their wealth in productive ways that foster their own growth and the growth of others. Material possessions, marriage and sexual intimacy, work, money, and positions of authority are just some of the opportunities life presents to live holy lives.

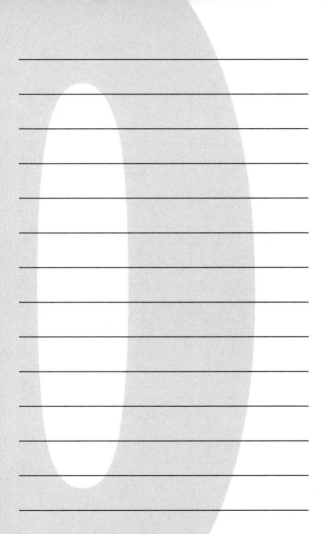

31 Holiness brings us to life. It refines every human ability. Holiness doesn't dampen our emotions; it elevates them. Those who respond to God's call to holiness are the most joyful people in history. They have a richer, more abundant experience of life, and they love more deeply than most people can ever imagine. They enjoy life, all of life. Even in the midst of suffering they are able to maintain a peace and a joy that are independent of the happenings and circumstances surrounding them. Holiness doesn't stifle us; it sets us free. The surest signs of holiness are not how often a person goes to church, how many hours he spends in prayer, what good spiritual books he has read, or even the number of good works he performs. The surest signs of holiness are an insatiable desire to become all God created us to be, an unwavering commitment to the will of God, and an unquenchable concern for unholy people. Living a holy life means letting our decisions be guided by the Holy Spirit. It means allowing each moment to be all it can be.

32 In any moment when you surrender to the will of God and choose to be the-best-version-of-yourself, you are holy. Any moment that you grasp as an opportunity to exercise virtue is a holy moment. But as quickly as this holiness can be found, it can be lost, because in any moment that you choose to be less than the-best-version-of-yourself, you have become distracted from living a holy life. There is nothing more attractive than holiness. This attractiveness has not only been demonstrated in Jesus, but is constantly demonstrated here and now in our own place and time: whenever someone goes out of his or her way to ease the burden of a stranger; whenever someone is honest; whenever someone lays down his or her life by working hard to support his or her family; whenever someone rejects the premise of modern culture. In his letter to the Thessalonians, Saint Paul writes, "This is the will of God: that you be saints." (1 Thessalonians 4:3) God wants you to be holy. Your holiness is the desire of God, the delight of God, and the source of your happiness. To embrace who you were created to be and to become the-best-version-of-yourself is God's dream for you. Therefore, holiness is for everyone, not just for a select few, for monks in monasteries and nuns in convents; it is for you and me.

Rediscover Catholicism

_____

_____

_____

_____

_____

_____

_____

_____

_____

_____

_____

_____

_____

_____

33 I believe there is a direct relationship between happiness and holiness. This was my first serious observation of the Christian life as a teenager. I must also confess it was the reason I first began to explore Catholicism seriously. As simple as it may sound, I was aware of my yearning for happiness. I had tried to satisfy this yearning in other ways and had been left wanting. I had witnessed a peace and purpose in the lives of a handful of people I knew who were striving to live their faith, and I knew they had something I was yearning for. God calls each of us to holiness. He invites us to be truly ourselves. This call to holiness is in response to our deep desire for happiness. We cry out to God, saying, *Show us how to find the happiness our hearts are hungry for,* and God replies, *Walk with me, be all I created you to be, become the-best-version-of-yourself.* It is a natural and logical conclusion that we will never find happiness if we are not ourselves.

_____

_____

_____

_____

_____

_____

_____

_____

_____

_____

_____

_____

34 The philosophy of Christ is based on discipline, and it is discipline that our modern culture abhors and has rejected with all its strength. It is true that Jesus came to comfort the afflicted, but as Dorothy Day, journalist, social activist, and Catholic convert pointed out, he also came to afflict the comfortable. The saints make many modern Catholics uncomfortable because they challenge us to throw off the spirit of the world and to embrace the Spirit of God. Like Jesus, by their example the saints invite us to a life of discipline. Contrary to popular opinion, discipline doesn't stifle or restrict the human person. Discipline isn't something invented by the Church to control or manipulate the masses, nor is it the tool that unjust tyrants and dictators use to make people do things they don't want to do. All these are the lies of a culture completely absorbed in a philosophy of instant gratification. Discipline is the faithful friend who will introduce you to your true self. Discipline is the worthy protector who will defend you from your lesser self. And discipline is the extraordinary mentor who will challenge you to become the-best-version-of-yourself and all God created you to be. What are your habits? Are your habits helping you become a-better-version-of-yourself or are they self-diminishing?

Rediscover Catholicism

35 The saints were remarkable men and women, but surprisingly what made them remarkable was rarely anything too spectacular. What made them extraordinary was the ordinary. They strove to grow in virtue through the ordinary things of everyday life. If they were caring for the sick they were growing in humility. When they were educating children they were growing in patience. As Saint Therese of Lisieux. said, "Do the little things with great love." There is nothing more attractive than holiness. Throughout history, wherever men and women of holiness have lived, the Church has blossomed. This is the answer to all of our questions and the solution to all of our problems: holiness of life. What are you willing to live for? Just before her death, Joan of Arc wrote, "I know this now. Every man gives his life for what he believes. Every woman gives her life for what she believes. Sometimes people believe in little or nothing, and yet they give their lives to that little or nothing. One life is all we have, and we live it as we believe in living it and then it's gone. But to surrender what you are and to live without belief is more terrible than dying—even more terrible than dying young." What are you willing to give your life for?

36 Within each of us there is a light. It is the light of God, and when it shines it reflects not only the wonder of God but also the greatness of the human spirit. We live in difficult times. I pray that we never become fearful, but rather we turn our focus to nurturing the light within us. I hope we allow that light within us to be nourished and to grow. Darkness has one enemy that it can never defeat, and that is light. Let your light shine! The best thing you can do for yourself is to become the-best-version-of-yourself. The best thing you can do for your spouse, your children, your friends, your Church, your nation, and God is to become the-best-version-of-yourself.

_____

_____

_____

_____

_____

_____

_____

_____

_____

_____

_____

_____

37 Catholicism is not a lifeless set of rules and regulations; it is a life-style. Catholicism is a dynamic way of life designed by God to help you explore your incredible potential.

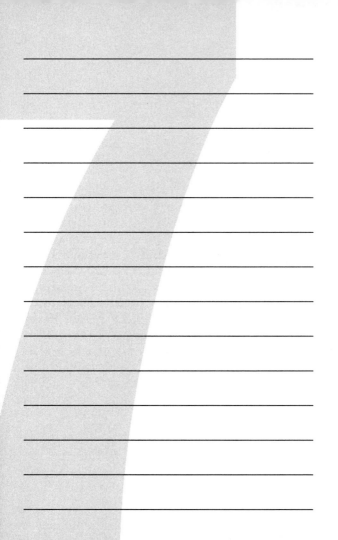

_____

_____

_____

_____

_____

_____

_____

_____

_____

_____

_____

_____

_____

38 Yesterday I was visiting a friend in Atlanta. He lives in a beautiful neighborhood and as we drove past these magnificent homes, one after another, I began to ask myself, "If your spiritual life were a house, what would it be like?" I would like to place the question before you now. If *your* spiritual life were a house, what would it be like? What street would it be on? What part of town would it be in? What would it look like? Would it be a house or a home? Is it in need of renovations? Is it peaceful, noisy, distracting, well organized, messy?

39 My favorite passage from the *Catechism of the Catholic Church* appears as the first line of the first chapter, and it reads, "The desire for God is written in the human heart, because man is created by God and for God; and God never ceases to draw man to himself. Only in God will he find the truth and happiness he never stops searching for."

40 A tree with deep roots can weather any storm. In your life and mine it is only a matter of time before the next storm gets here: an illness, the death of a loved one, unemployment, financial difficulties, a troubled child, a natural disaster, marital strife, or any number of other things. The storms of life are inevitable. The question is not whether there will be another storm. The question is: When will the next storm get here? And when the next storm gets here, it's too late to sink the roots. When the next storm gets here, you either have the roots or you don't.

41 This process of identifying strengths and weaknesses and transforming weaknesses into strengths is classic Catholic spirituality. For two thousand years, the champions of Christianity, the men and women we call saints, have been going into the classroom of silence, taking a humble and honest look at themselves, and assessing their own strengths and weaknesses. Then, armed with this knowledge, they have bravely set forth to transform their weaknesses into strengths, their vices into virtues.

_____

_____

_____

_____

_____

_____

_____

_____

_____

_____

_____

_____

42 *Repent* is a powerful word. But what does it mean for you and me, here and now, more than two thousand years later? It means the same as it did to the people walking around the dusty pathways in their sandals, trying to inch closer to Jesus as he passed through their town or village. *Repent* means "to turn back to God." I find myself needing to turn back to God many times a day, in ways small and large. It is not a matter of guilt and it is not a shameful thing. It is simply that at his side I am a better person—a better son, husband, father, brother, friend, employer, and citizen. Over time, I have also come to realize, quite painfully, that when I turn away from God I am also turning my back on my true self. Do you need to turn back to God today? Do you need to repent?

43 I am a sinner and I need to be saved. I need to be saved from myself and from my sin. There are many people who love me deeply—parents, siblings, friends, colleagues, and neighbors—but they cannot save me. I need a savior. It is the clarity of this realization that is life changing. This is what makes me eligible for membership in the Catholic Church. Jesus didn't come for the healthy; he came for the sick, and he established the Church to continue his work (cf. Mark 2:17). I am imperfect, but I am capable of change and growth. We are all imperfect but perfectible. The Church holds me in my weakness, comforts me in my limitations, endeavors to heal me of my sickness, and nurtures me back to full health, making me whole again. And throughout this process, the Church manages to harness all my efforts and struggles, not only for my own good, but for the good of the entire Church and indeed humanity. This is just a tiny part of the incredible mystery of the Church.

44 Grace is the power of God alive within us. It heals the wounds that our sins have created and helps us to maintain moral balance. Grace helps us to persevere in the pursuit of virtue. It enlightens our minds to see and know which actions will help us become all God has created us to be. Grace inspires us to love what is good and shun what is evil. Grace is not a magical illusion. It is mystical and real. I come to Confession to reconcile with myself, with God, and with the community. Confession is not just a cleansing experience; it is also a strengthening experience. Confession is an opportunity for you and God to work together to form a-better-version-of-yourself. It also increases our desire for holiness, and that is a desire we should fan with all our energy.

45 The truth is, I do things every day that are contrary to the ways of God, things that stop me from being the-best-version-of-myself, and so do you—every day. Then we carry all this baggage around with us and it affects us in ways that we are often not even aware of. Our sins affect us physically, emotionally, intellectually, spiritually, and psychologically. They affect our relationships, our work, our health, our intellectual clarity, and our ability to genuinely embrace and experience all of life. Sin limits our future by chaining us to the past. Yet, most people are able to convince themselves either that sin doesn't exist, that they don't sin, or that their sins are not affecting them. But if we take an honest inventory of our thoughts, words, and actions, it becomes abundantly clear that every one of us does things that are self-destructive, offensive to others, contrary to the natural laws of the universe, and in direct conflict with the ways of God. If we really think we can carry all this around inside us and that it is not affecting us, then we are only deceiving ourselves.

46 Prayer is central to the Christian experience. A Christian life is not sustainable without it, because growth in the Christian life is simply not possible without prayer. Growing in character and virtue, learning to hear the voice of God in our lives and walking where he calls us—all require the discipline of prayer. And it is not enough simply to pray when we feel like it. Prayer requires a daily commitment. Get to know the Shepherd. Stop trying to put together a master plan for your life and for your happiness. Instead, seek out the Master's plan for your life and for your happiness. Allow him to lead you, to guide you, to be your companion, your friend, your coach, and your mentor. He will lead you to green pastures. He will restore your soul. And your cup will overflow.

47 Mass is not about whom you sit next to. It's not about which priest says Mass. It is not about what you wear or who is there. Mass is not about the music. It's not even about the preaching. It about gathering as a community to give thanks to God for all the blessings he fills our lives with. It is about receiving the body and blood of Christ, not just physically, but spiritually. Perhaps you have been receiving the Eucharist physically every Sunday for your whole life. Next Sunday, prepare yourself, be conscious of the marvel, the wonder, the mystery, and receive spiritually.

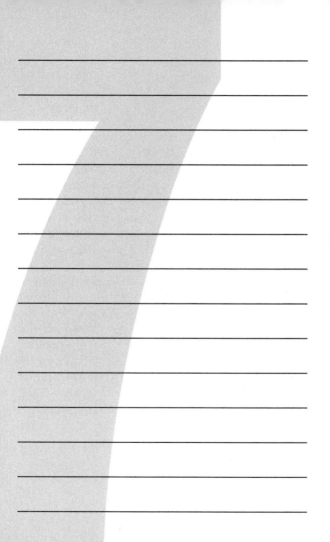

_____

_____

_____

_____

_____

_____

_____

_____

_____

_____

_____

_____

_____

48 Three or four years ago, my brother Andrew gave me a copy of a book titled *Letters to a Young Poet*. It is a small book that contains a collection of letters written by the great German lyric poet Rainer Maria Rilke to Franz Kappus, who at the time was a young aspiring poet. In one of the letters, Rilke penned some words that have remained ingrained on my heart since I read and underlined them in that small volume: "Be patient toward all that is unresolved in your heart and try to love the questions themselves like locked rooms and like books that are written in a foreign tongue. Do not now seek the answers, which cannot be given you because you would not be able to live them. And the point is, to live everything. Live the questions now. Perhaps you will then gradually, without noticing it, live along some distant day into the answer."

_____

_____

_____

_____

_____

_____

_____

_____

_____

_____

_____

_____

49 There is genius in Catholicism. The human heart yearns for happiness, and God wants us to be happy. But we only experience this happiness, and the fulfillment that accompanies it, when we are changing, growing, becoming more like Jesus Christ and through him becoming the-best-version-of-ourselves. Catholicism is the dynamic lifestyle and learning system divinely designed to assist us in this transformation. I love the Church. To me, Catholicism is a gift that can never be fully appreciated, described, or understood. But in order to even begin to appreciate Catholicism in all its beauty we must experience it. My travels have affirmed that people love the Church. The press may attack the Church, fallen-away Catholics may ridicule it, and even practicing Catholics may criticize it, but I firmly believe these are curious expressions of love. At the very least, they are expressions of a desire for the Church to be the beacon of light it should be in the world. Sometimes love goes sour, as it has for many modern Catholics in their relationship with the Church. When love goes sour, it is usually for one of four reasons: misunderstanding, indifference, selfishness, or the pride that makes a person unwilling to apologize or forgive. Sometimes it is a combination, and usually both parties are at fault to some extent.

Rediscover Catholicism

50 If the Catholic Church is to change, grow, thrive, and fulfill its mission in this modern climate, it will be for one reason: because we become a more spiritual people. Only then will this renewed spiritual health burst forth into authentic action. It would seem to me that education and evangelization are the keys to helping the whole Church to blossom. They are the pillars of renewal. It is impossible to know God and not love him. It is equally impossible to experience God and not want others to experience him as a result. Those who do not evangelize simply have not had an intimate experience of God. If you went into an ice cream parlor and there was no ice cream, you'd say, "There's a problem!" If you went to a chocolate shop and there was no chocolate, you'd say, "There's a problem!" The mission of the Church is to share the Gospel, and to teach, encourage, and challenge people to become more like Jesus Christ. So how is it that we can belong to a local church community that goes on year after year with almost no outreach to the unchurched and underchurched in the area, with very few people becoming markedly more Christ-like, and not think there is a problem? Let me tell you, if this describes your church community, *there's a problem!*

51 The early Church was unstoppable, and as far as I can tell, it was because they followed this simple strategy. They believed that the values and principles of the Gospel were the best way to live. They nurtured friendships. They were deeply committed to a life of prayer. They were courageous in telling their story. They were generous and welcoming. Friendship is the original model of evangelization, and it is the model that will triumph in the modern context. Friendship establishes trust and mutual respect, which together bring about the openness and acceptance that give birth to vulnerable dialogue. Only then can we begin addressing the questions that every human heart longs to answer: Who am I? Where did I come from? What am I here for? How do I do it? Where am I going? Friendship is the key to evangelization.

52 Does it not strike you as a great poverty of leadership that here in America we cannot put one person on the evening news who can be acknowledged by Americans from coast to coast as a Catholic leader? Where is the "someone" who speaks for us? It is true that occasionally a bishop or cardinal effectively harnesses the media in his diocese and establishes a vibrant identity as a Catholic leader in his geographic area. It is also true that some lay Catholics who occupy positions of prominence in the business world, the entertainment world, or the political realm have successfully established a Catholic identity in different ways. But we have no national figures, not within the clergy and not among the laity. Does that not strike you as a massive poverty of leadership? Where is the Catholic leader who can speak to the people of our time in ways that are bold, brilliant, logical, articulate, and inspiring?

_____

_____

_____

_____

_____

_____

_____

_____

_____

_____

_____

_____

_____

The most dominant emotion in our modern society is fear. We are afraid—afraid of losing the things we have worked hard to buy, afraid of rejection and failure, afraid of certain parts of town, afraid of certain types of people, afraid of criticism, of suffering and heartache, of change, afraid to tell people how we really feel. We are afraid of so many things. We are even afraid to be ourselves. Some of these fears we are consciously aware of, while others exist subconsciously. But all these fears play a large role in directing the actions and activities of our lives. Fear has a tendency to imprison us. Fear stops more people from doing something incredible with their lives than lack of ability, contacts, resources, or any other single variable. Fear paralyzes the human spirit.

NOTES

_____

_____

_____

_____

_____

_____

_____

_____

_____

_____

_____

Everything in life requires courage. Whether it is playing or coaching football, crossing the room to ask a girl out on a date or rekindling a love that has grown cold, starting a new business, battling a potentially fatal disease, getting married, struggling to overcome an addiction, or coming humbly before your God in prayer, life requires courage. Courage is essential to the human experience. It animates us, brings us to life, and makes everything else possible. And yet, courage is the rarest quality in a human person. The measure of your life will be the measure of your courage.

NOTES

_____

_____

_____

_____

_____

_____

_____

_____

_____

_____

_____

What we need is bold leadership. Goethe, the famous German author, once wrote, "Be bold and mighty forces will come to your aid." It is this boldness that the Church needs. And I promise you that whenever and wherever a leader emerges with this boldness, the people will clamor to support such leadership. They will respond like people dying of thirst who have just been offered a cool drink of water. It will be as true for a local pastor in his parish as it was for John Paul II on an international scale. The people are desperate for authentic leadership. They are lost and lonely, like sheep without a shepherd. People don't follow titles and authority. They follow courage.

NOTES

_____

_____

_____

_____

_____

_____

_____

_____

_____

_____

_____

Eight hundred years ago, a young Italian man searching for meaning in his life went into a dilapidated old church and heard the voice of God speak to him: "Rebuild my Church. As you can see, it is in ruins." If you and I listen carefully, I believe we will hear the same voice saying the same thing in our hearts today.

Rediscover Catholicism

NOTES

_____

_____

_____

_____

_____

_____

_____

_____

_____

_____

_____

_____

The only way for our lives to genuinely improve is by acquiring virtue. Similarly, it is
impossible for a society to genuinely improve
unless its members grow in virtue. The renewal that the Church so desperately needs
is a renewal of virtue. And it is our relationship with Christ that gives us the strength, the
grace, and the wisdom to grow in virtue. What
is virtue? It is "the habitual and form disposi-
tion to do good." (CCC #1833) The great
fallacy of the lukewarm moral life is to believe
that our sole responsibility is to eliminate vice
from our lives. In the absence of a sincere and
focused effort to grow in virtue and an openness to God's will for our lives, vice will creep
into our lives in the form of a hundred different self-centered and self-destructive habits. No man or woman is born virtuous. Good
habits are not infused. Virtue must be sought
out and can be acquired only by continual
practice. You learn to ride a bicycle by riding
a bicycle. You learn to be patient by practicing
patience. You become virtuous by practicing
virtue. The connection between virtue and the
flourishing of an individual is unquestionable.
To live a life of virtue is to move beyond the
chaos and restlessness that agonize the human heart, and embrace a life of coherence.
Similarly, the relationship between the virtue
of the members of a community and the flourishing of their society is proven time and time
again throughout history.

NOTES

_____

_____

_____

_____

_____

_____

_____

_____

_____

_____

_____

_____

The Catholic Church feeds, clothes, houses, and educates more people than any other organization in the world. And when the modern media and the secular culture have finished tearing down the Church as best they can, let me ask you, who will take our place? Who will feed the hungry? Who will clothe the naked? Who will visit the lonely and imprisoned? Who will house the homeless? Who will comfort the sick and dying? Who will educate the masses? The world needs the Church. Even your hardened and cynical politicians with nothing in mind but personal gain recognize this reality with alarming clarity. If for no other reason than from an economic standpoint, they know they wouldn't be able to pick up the broken pieces that would be left if the Church disappeared from their community.

NOTES

_____

_____

_____

_____

_____

_____

_____

_____

_____

_____

_____

We should try not to forget that when Jesus was on the cross, he didn't turn to the man next to him and say, "You did the crime, now pay the price." No, he offered him a better life. That is the responsibility that now falls on our shoulders as followers of Jesus – to offer people a better life.

NOTES

_____

_____

_____

_____

_____

_____

_____

_____

_____

_____

_____

_____

Hope is a good thing, maybe the best of things. Hope is one of those things that you can't buy, but that will be freely given to you if you ask. Hope is the one thing people cannot live without. Hope is a thing of beauty. I hope. I hope I can live up to the gifts and talents God has given me. I hope I can have the courage to be a true friend, a good father, and a loving husband. I hope I never stop striving to become the-best-version-of-myself. I hope I will continue to take time to listen to the voice of God each day. I hope I will have the courage to follow where his voice leads me. I hope we can build a world where our children can grow free and strong. I hope . . . and that is a wonderful thing. Join me in that hope and together we will awaken all men and women to discover the incredible dream God has for their lives and for the world.

NOTES

_____

_____

_____

_____

_____

_____

_____

_____

_____

_____

_____

_____

_____

_____

NOTES

_____

_____

_____

_____

_____

_____

_____

_____

_____

_____

_____

_____

_____

Rediscover Catholicism

NOTES

_____

_____

_____

_____

_____

_____

_____

_____

_____

_____

_____

_____

NOTES

_____

_____

_____

_____

_____

_____

_____

_____

_____

_____

_____

Rediscover Catholicism

NOTES

_____

_____

_____

_____

_____

_____

_____

_____

_____

_____

_____

_____

NOTES

_____

_____

_____

_____

_____

_____

_____

_____

_____

_____

_____

_____

Rediscover Catholicism

NOTES

_____

_____

_____

_____

_____

_____

_____

_____

_____

_____

_____

_____

NOTES

_____

_____

_____

_____

_____

_____

_____

_____

_____

_____

_____

_____

NOTES

NOTES

_____

_____

_____

_____

_____

_____

_____

_____

_____

_____

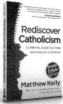

Rediscover Catholicism
Matthew Kelly

Get a FREE copy at **DynamicCatholic.com**
Shipping and handling not included.

NOTES

_____

_____

_____

_____

_____

_____

_____

_____

_____

_____

NOTES

_____

_____

_____

_____

_____

_____

_____

_____

_____

_____

Life's Greatest Lesson
Allen Hunt

Get a FREE* copy at **DynamicCatholic.com**
*Shipping and handling not included.

NOTES

_____

_____

_____

_____

_____

_____

_____

_____

_____

_____

The Real Story
Curtis Martin & Edward Sri

Get a FREE*copy at **DynamicCatholic.com**
*Shipping and handling not included.

THE
PRAYER PROCESS

1. **GRATITUDE:** Begin by thanking God in a personal dialogue for whatever you are most grateful for today.

2. **AWARENESS:** Revisit the times in the past twenty-four hours when you were and were not the-best-version-of-yourself. Talk to God about these situations and what you learned from them.

3. **SIGNIFICANT MOMENTS:** Identify something you experienced in the last twenty-four hours and explore what God might be trying to say to you through that event (or person).

4. **PEACE:** Ask God to forgive you for any wrong you have committed (against yourself, another person, or Him) and to fill you with a deep and abiding peace.

5. **FREEDOM:** Speak with God about how He is inviting you to change your life, so that you can experience the freedom to be the-best-version-of-yourself.

6. **OTHERS:** Lift up to God anyone you feel called to pray for today, asking God to bless and guide them.

7. Pray the **OUR FATHER.**

THE
DYNAMIC CATHOLIC
INSTITUTE

[MISSION]

To re-energize the Catholic Church
in America by developing world-class
resources that inspire people to
rediscover the genius of Catholicism.

[VISION]

To be the innovative leader in the
New Evangelization helping Catholics
and their parishes become
the-best-version-of-themselves.

DynamicCatholic.com
Be Bold. Be Catholic.®

The Dynamic Catholic Institute
5081 Olympic Blvd
Erlanger, Kentucky 41018
Phone: 859–980–7900
Email: info@DynamicCatholic.com